GLOBAL CITIZENSHIP

Understanding Human Rights

A⁺

S U S A N   W A T S O N

This edition first published in 2004 in the United States of America by Smart Apple Media.

Smart Apple Media
1980 Lookout Drive
North Mankato
Minnesota 56003

Library of Congress Cataloging-in-Publication Data

Watson, Susan, 1949–
    Understanding human rights / by Susan Watson.
    p. cm — (Global citizenship)

    Includes index.
    Summary: Explores the basic needs of human beings, why they are not met in some parts of the world, how war and politics impact human rights, and what can be done to help meet people's basic needs, both through such groups as the United Nations and the efforts of individual citizens.

    ISBN 1-58340-402-3
    1. Human rights—Juvenile literature. 2. Children's rights—Juvenile literature. 3. World citizenship—Juvenile literature. 4. Globalization—Juvenile literature. [1. Human rights. 2. Childrens' rights. 3. World citizenship. 4. Globalization.] I. Title.
    JC571.W28 2003
    323—dc21   20020044617

First Edition
9 8 7 6 5 4 3 2 1

First published in 2003 by
MACMILLAN EDUCATION AUSTRALIA PTY LTD
627 Chapel Street, South Yarra, Australia 3141

Associated companies and representatives throughout the world.

Packaged for Macmillan Education Australia by Publishing Options Pty Ltd
Text design by Gail McManus Graphics
Cover design by Dimitrios Frangoulis
Illustrations by Infographics Pty Ltd
Page make-up by Crackerjack Desktop Services

Printed in Thailand

Acknowledgements
The author is especially grateful to Matthew, Kyja, CJ, and Samantha for being the model global citizens of this series. The author and the publisher are grateful to the following for permission to reproduce copyright materials:

Cover photograph: young refugees, courtesy of Reuters.

AAP/AFP Photo/Hoang Dinh Nam, p. 9; ANT Photo Library, p. 16; Kevin Hamdorf/Auscape International, p. 8; Mike Langford/Auscape International, p. 7 (top right); Australian Picture Library/ Corbis, pp. 7 (center), 11 (left), 29 (top), 29 (center); Coo-ee Picture Library, pp. 25 (bottom), 29 (bottom); Getty Images, pp. 12, 13, 15 (top), 27 top; Newspix/AFP Photo/Toru Yamanaka, p. 10 (top); Newspix/Dean Martin, p. 20; Reuters, pp. 4–5 (center), 11 (right), 18, 19, 22 (bottom), 25 (top), 28 (top); logo used with permission of the UN, p. 22 (top); logo used with permission of UNHCR, p. 21; Susan Watson, pp. 4 (far left), 4 (center left), 5 (center right), 5 (far right), 6, 7 (left), 17 (center), 30; World Vision, pp. 21 (top), 24.

While every care has been taken to trace and acknowledge copyright, the publisher tenders their apologies for any accidental infringement where copyright has proved untraceable. Where the attempt has been unsuccessful, the publisher welcomes information that would redress the situation.

Please note
At the time of printing, the Internet addresses appearing in this book were correct. Owing to the dynamic nature of the Internet, however, we cannot guarantee that all these addresses will remain correct.

Contents

Global citizens

citizen
a person who lives in a large group of people who they mix with

rights
fair claims to things in daily life

responsibilities
duties that have to be done

environments
natural and built surroundings

A global citizen is a person who:
◎ has rights and responsibilities
◎ acts in a caring way based on knowledge and understanding
◎ relates to others within their family, friendship groups, community, and country
◎ develops personal values and commitments
◎ develops a sense of their own role in the world.

A study of global citizenship will help you understand how people affect the quality of global environments and the well-being of others. Active global citizens do not just sit back and wait for others to do something. They turn their ideas into action. Action can take many forms:
◎ volunteering by giving time, help, and ideas freely
◎ talking to your friends
◎ thinking deeply
◎ learning more
◎ taking part in community events.

Throughout this book Allira, Harry, Lin, and Denzel will tell you their ways of acting as global citizens. We can all care for each other and our environment.

ALLIRA

Hi! I'm Allira. I live in a country town near the sea. My family background is Aboriginal–Australian.

we are global citizens

HARRY

Hello. I'm Harry. I live with my family in a suburb of a big modern city of four million people.

Learning about human rights, especially the rights of children, will help you understand that:

◎ all people belong to the human race and they deserve to be treated with respect
◎ belonging to a particular group does not make a person better than others
◎ everybody has basic needs
◎ the needs of many of the world's people are not being met
◎ global citizens are concerned when the needs of other people are not being met.

There are global issues facing millions of the world's children and older people too. Some of these might be happening in your own country.

Each of us can learn to understand human rights through thinking about and discussing issues that affect everyone. We can act on ideas by working together.

human rights
the basic claims that all people have to fair, safe, and comfortable lives

needs
the things that people must have to stay alive

The human rights of many of the world's young people are not being met. These children have been forced to leave their homes and wait in a camp outside their country.

LIN

I'm Lin. I migrated to my new country with my parents. We live with my grandparents who came 15 years ago from Malaysia.

DENZEL

We are global citizens

Hi! I'm Denzel. My mom and I live in a high-rise apartment close to the city center. We're African-American.

Things people need to live

All people have basic needs. Not having them met will affect how they live and grow. People also have wants, but having these met is not essential. The most basic of human needs are:

◎ fresh, safe water
◎ nutritious food
◎ satisfactory housing and clothing
◎ love and self-esteem
◎ a sense of freedom and safety from harm.

Young children also have the need to play and learn.

Fresh and safe water

All living things on Earth need water. The water must be fresh, not salty, and safe for drinking. We cannot drink freshwater that has been polluted with chemicals or waste.

People also need places to store freshwater. We build tanks, dams, wells, pipes, and irrigation ditches for water storage.

Freshwater is not evenly spread over the world. There are places that get very little rainfall and have no large rivers or lakes. There are also many polluted rivers and storage dams. This means that all people do not have the same access to fresh and safe water.

Nutritious food

If people do not have enough healthy food they become hungry. Hunger can lead to starvation. Nutritious food gives a person enough energy, vitamins, and minerals for them to be healthy.

However, not all people can get proper food. It is often of poor quality and not nutritious enough to help them grow strong. This can lead to malnutrition.

wants
the things that people like to have to make their life comfortable, but are not essential

self-esteem
the feelings a person has about their own value

freedom
the right to choose

starvation
suffering or death because of lack of food

malnutrition
an illness caused by not having enough healthy food

GLOBAL FACT
The world grows and makes enough food to feed all of the world's people.

Access to healthy food and fresh, safe water are two of the basic human needs.

Housing and clothing

People have a basic need for adequate housing that provides satisfactory shelter. People also need clothing to protect them from the cold and heat.

Some people's homes are not adequate. They might be made of poor materials, have poor sanitation, and be very cramped.

People who do not have any shelter are said to be "homeless." Young people who are homeless and live outside in parks and on the street are called "street kids." There are homeless people in most countries.

shelter
a place, like a house, that gives people protection from the weather

sanitation
clean and safe removal of human waste by water and drains

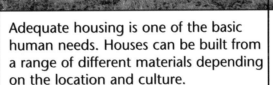

Adequate housing is one of the basic human needs. Houses can be built from a range of different materials depending on the location and culture.

Other basic needs

The other basic needs cannot be seen or touched. They are feelings. People need to:
◎ be loved by others
◎ have good self-esteem
◎ have the freedom to live as responsible citizens in their community
◎ think for themselves
◎ be able to choose friends and activities for themselves
◎ be safe from harm.

What can I do?
I'm going to brainstorm "needs" and "wants" with my classmates. We'll list the things that we need to grow up healthy and safe, and the things that add to a comfortable life. We'll make two lists on the board and discuss them.

Why are basic needs not met?

Many people are not having their needs satisfied:

◎ about 20 percent of the world's people do not have safe drinking water or proper sanitation

◎ about 12 million people die of hunger every year

◎ at least 25 percent of all people do not have adequate housing

◎ more than 100 million people are homeless.

Poverty

Poverty is the main reason that people's basic needs are not being met. Poverty means that:

◎ people cannot afford to buy enough healthy food

◎ they do not have enough money to own land and build adequate housing

◎ local communities do not have enough money to provide good services such as water supply and waste removal

◎ some richer people use poorer people to work for them at very low rates of pay.

Just think of all the things that a family does in a day in a typical household in a rich country like the United States. If you add up the cost spent by the family, it would be at least $45 for the day. Yet half the world's families live on less than 10 percent of this— $4.50 per day.

poverty
extreme lack of money or wealth

shanty town
an area of very poor housing conditions next to better housing in a city

This is a shanty town of houses made of poor materials. The houses do not provide good shelter and sanitation.

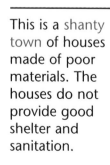

Overcrowding and pollution

More and more people are crowding into huge cities. Many have lived in poor farming areas. They move to cities in search of work and a better life. However, they are often forced to live in overcrowded housing with poor sanitation. The streets and water supply are often polluted. Sometimes people have to walk a long way just to collect a small amount of daily water.

Conditions of overcrowding and pollution spoil people's chances of getting freshwater and adequate housing.

Disasters and war

Natural disasters happen all over the world from time to time. There are earthquakes, hurricanes, blizzards, and volcanic eruptions. Buildings are destroyed. People are injured and die.

When disaster hits the poorer areas of the world, the effects are often worse than in richer countries. Hundreds or thousands of people could be left with ruined homes, polluted water supplies, and a shortage of food. Sometimes children are left with no parents and can become homeless.

War is a threat to people's needs in the same way that natural disasters are. War destroys homes, kills people, and makes others homeless. War damages farmland and water supplies.

overcrowding
a large number of people living in a very small area in cramped conditions

pollution
dirty or dangerous conditions that make a part of the environment unclean or unsafe

Earthquakes can damage people's housing and supply of water.

Basic needs are basic human rights

Think about the things that you and your family do every day in your own community. Everyone has certain rights from living in a community. Some rights that many people have are:

◎ the right to own pets
◎ the right to drive a car once they reach a certain age and pass a driving test
◎ the right to go to work and earn money
◎ the right to own land, to build a house on it, and to live in it
◎ the right not to be the victim of violence or torture
◎ the right to meet in groups to discuss things freely.

torture
extreme cruelty

These examples are part of the basic needs people have for freedom and proper housing.

All people are entitled to all of the basic human needs, regardless of their backgrounds. This is known as human rights. Each person has human rights as a citizen of a particular society. Human rights are part of everyday life. Without human rights people cannot have self-esteem as human beings. Human rights are the basis of freedom, fairness, and peace.

In some countries, people are the victims of torture. Torture is a crime against human rights. This Japanese girl is protesting against torture.

What can I do?
Our teacher has asked us to watch TV news and read newspapers over the next month. We have to find information about people who are not being given their human rights. We'll discuss this in class.

What human rights mean for you

From the beginning of your life until the end, human rights are your rights. You are entitled to your human rights simply because you are a person. You do not have to buy them, earn them, or have them passed down to you from another generation.

These rights stay yours, regardless of:

◎ where you live
◎ what you believe
◎ how you look
◎ who you parents are
◎ whatever is happening in the community or world around you.

No one has the right to take your human rights away from you. You are entitled to live in dignity. You have the right to freedom, safety, and a decent standard of living, all at the same time.

What applies to you and your human rights also applies to everybody else. Whatever differences there might be between you and other people, you share the very same human rights. Human rights are common to all peoples of the world.

Protecting human rights

The United Nations is an international organization. It was started at the end of World War II in 1945 to help the world keep peace. Nearly all the countries of the world are members of it. The United Nations is concerned for all people in all countries. It tries to protect the human rights of all the world's people.

generation
people of about the same age group and living at the same time

dignity
respecting yourself

standard of living
everyday living conditions in a community

United Nations
a worldwide organization that aims to protect peace and human rights

international
worldwide

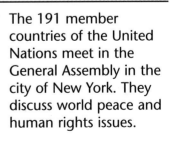

Kofi Annan is the Secretary-General of the United Nations. He often appears in the media.

The 191 member countries of the United Nations meet in the General Assembly in the city of New York. They discuss world peace and human rights issues.

The United Nations protects children's rights

The United Nations decided that children have some special rights as part of their human rights. These special rights are because children are young and need protection.

The United Nations helps protect children's rights and human rights by asking the countries of the world to sign important documents. These are like international law. One document is called a declaration, the other type of document is a convention.

A declaration of children's rights

In 1957, the United Nations made its first document about children's rights called the "Declaration of the Rights of the Child." This document asked the world's countries to stand up for the special rights of children. The actual document is long and has difficult language. There are 10 main points.

law
rules that must be obeyed

declaration
a document that countries agree to but do not have to make law

convention
a document that countries agree to and must make the law

gender
whether a person is male (boy, man) or female (girl, woman)

politics
the groups who control and run a country

All children have equal human rights, regardless of their backgrounds.

DECLARATION OF THE RIGHTS OF THE CHILD

1. The right to be equal to all others, regardless of race, color, gender, language, religion, politics, or national or social group.
2. The right to grow up in a normal and healthy way—free and with self-esteem.
3. The right to have a name and be a citizen of a country.
4. The right to good food, housing, and medical care.
5. The right to special care if disabled in any way.
6. The right to love and understanding, preferably from parents.
7. The right to go to school for free up to the age of 15, to play, and to have an equal chance to learn to be a responsible and useful citizen.
8. The right to be among the first to be protected when there is harm.
9. The right not to be harmed or to be made to go to work until old enough.
10. The right to be brought up in a world of peace and friendship.

A convention on children's rights

Countries that agree to a convention must make the points in the convention become the law. In 1989, the United Nations made its second document about children's rights called the "Convention on the Rights of the Child." This document asked the world's countries to make the rights of children the law for all their citizens. Nearly every country in the world has agreed to the convention.

The convention has four important features:

◎ it lists all children's rights in one document
◎ it makes adults see children as individuals with rights
◎ it applies to all children and young people everywhere
◎ it covers the full range of human rights.

The convention says that a child is a person under the age of 18. A child is an individual as well as a member of a family and a community. A child is a human being with the full range of rights.

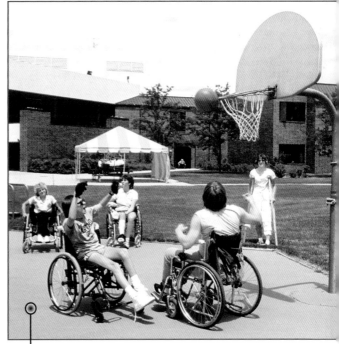

These young people have equal human rights to those with stronger physical abilities.

SUMMARY OF THE CONVENTION ON THE RIGHTS OF THE CHILD

1 Every child must be officially registered immediately after birth in the country of birth. They should be given a name and nationality, and grow up knowing who their parents or nearest family members are.
2 Every child has the same rights as every other child no matter what their nationality, skin color, gender, language, religion, political views, or social group.
3 Every child must live free from situations that cause early death or disability, and be protected from dangerous work or being made to fight in an army at an early age.
4 Every child must be protected from all forms of physical and mental violence and poor care, even from families. Special child protection should be made available for children not treated properly.
5 Every child must be protected from using, making, and distributing drugs.
6 Every child must be safe from being sold or used for sexual reasons.
7 Every child has the right to go to elementary school at least, and where possible, high school to develop their talents and to enable them to become a responsible adult in the future.

The right to education

A free and basic schooling to the age of 15 is every child's right. These are the special human rights that relate to education:

◎ Children without money are entitled to an education.

◎ All girls, as well as boys, are entitled to an education.

◎ Children who must work to support their families are entitled to an education.

◎ Children with disabilities are entitled to an education.

◎ Children affected by violence, conflict, or disease are entitled to an education.

◎ Schools should be places where all boys and girls feel safe and are supported in their learning.

Many of the world's children do not have access to education. This could be because:

◎ the community is too poor to pay for schools

◎ the only school is too far away from home

◎ the children are working to support their families

◎ there is war

◎ the children have diseases and are too sick to go to school.

Education is also a responsibility

Education is not only a child's right. It is also a child's responsibility. It is one of the most important responsibilities a child can undertake. Education helps children learn and grow into responsible and useful citizens.

GLOBAL FACT

Today, more than 110 million school-age children worldwide are not going to school. Girls make up 80 million of these children.

conflict
violent disagreement

This bar chart shows the differences in children's access to education. Many children are not able to attend high school.

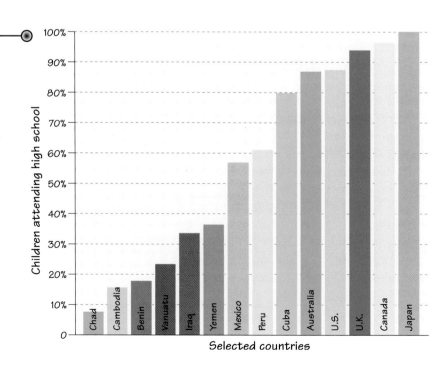

Children attending high school

Chad, Cambodia, Benin, Vanuatu, Iraq, Yemen, Mexico, Peru, Cuba, Australia, U.S., U.K., Canada, Japan

Selected countries

The right to play

Play is a very important part in all children's lives. Play helps children understand the world by learning new things. Play helps them learn to:

◎ follow instructions
◎ pay attention
◎ solve problems
◎ be patient
◎ stick at something until it is finished
◎ get along with other people
◎ deal with their emotions
◎ use their muscles to become coordinated and strong
◎ act out their thoughts and feelings.

Children also have the right to some spare time. They need to be able to relax and join in sporting, artistic, and cultural activities. Children have the right to enjoy at least a few hours every day when they are free from worries.

These rights help children grow into healthy adult citizens.

Play is important to a child's healthy growth. The right to play is a right of all children everywhere.

What can I do?

I've noticed that the two new kids down the street hardly ever get out to play. They live in an apartment just with their mom. She's always busy working or cleaning. I'm going to ask them over to play in our backyard.

Children forced to work

Nearly all the countries of the world have agreed to the United Nation's "Convention on the Rights of the Child." Yet, all of the world's children are not treated equally.

In some places, children are forced to go to work before they reach the age of 15. They not only have to work, but often the work is also hard and boring. The pay is usually very low, and where they work can be dangerous and unhealthy. This is known as child labor.

Some children are not paid at all but made to work as slaves. This can happen when children have lost their parents in war or through disease. Some parents who are very poor can be forced to give away their children in return for money.

child labor
where children under 15 are forced to work for low pay and in bad conditions

slaves
people who are owned by another, have no freedom, and must obey the owner

 **CASE STUDY** Anwar, a child slave

At the age of seven, Anwar and his sister, Gunal, started weaving carpets in a village in South Asia. They were given some food, very little rest time, and no medical care. They were told over and over again that they could not stop working until they earned enough money to pay back money that their family owed. Anwar was never told who in his family had borrowed the money nor how much had been borrowed.

When Anwar and Gunal made mistakes they were fined, so the amount owed got bigger. When they worked too slowly, they were beaten with a stick.

The carpets children like Anwar and Gunal make are sold all over the world and the factory owners are rich. Their rights as children have been taken away.

GLOBAL FACT
Over 50 million children under the age of 12 work in dangerous and unhealthy conditions.

16

Tourism can create child labor

Many poor countries rely on tourists for money. Tourists spend money on transportation, sightseeing, accommodation, and souvenirs. Sometimes tourists deal directly with child laborers.

How can global citizens help child laborers?

There are some things global citizens can do to help children who are forced to work at an early age and in bad conditions:

◎ Buy carpets and rugs only with a Rugmark label. This label shows that the rug has not been made by child labor.

◎ Volunteer your time to organizations working to protect children.

◎ Learn more about child labor and the laws against it.

◎ Call your friends together and form a group united against the problem.

◎ Make some posters or murals about child labor and display these at school or in another community place.

◎ Write down your thoughts on child labor and publish them on the Internet.

 CASE STUDY **Vung, a street seller**

Vung is 10 years old. He lives in the city of Ho Chi Minh in Vietnam. His family is very poor. Vung used to go to school in the mornings. After completing Grade 3 he was forced to leave school to help his parents make more money to live on. He shines shoes and sells cigarette lighters. Vung and a group of other children work for a man who gives them the goods to sell. They give him the money they earn. Only a very small amount of money is left for the child laborers.

Vung usually works 11 hours, from 8:00 A.M. to 7:00 P.M. After work, he goes to school three nights a week from 7:00 P.M. until 9:30 P.M. The school is run especially for poor children who work in the daytime. Vung likes school and misses going to school in the day.

What can I do?

Our class is going to raise some money to donate to an organization working for children's rights. We want to "adopt" a child laborer and help their family. Then the child can stay at school.

17

Children forced to fight

In many areas of the world where people are fighting one another, children are forced to become soldiers. They are given some basic training, and guns and other weapons. They sometimes live in army camps with older people who are not their family.

Child soldiers can be homeless orphans who lost their parents in a war. Other children are stolen from their families and forced to fight. They can be as young as 10 years old. Modern guns are now light enough for a 10-year-old child to carry and fire. Both boys and girls are used as soldiers, although there are fewer girls. Girls face extra suffering if they are treated badly by army men.

What happens to child soldiers?

landmines
bombs that have been hidden in the earth that will explode when stepped on

Child soldiers have had their human rights taken away. They get injured and killed more easily than adults. They are often used to lead adult troops across fields containing landmines.

Those who do not die in war suffer from their violent experience. They can have horrible memories for the rest of their lives because they have been forced to kill and torture other people. They are sometimes even forced to do these things to their own families.

After a war is over, child soldiers can be left physically disabled and mentally injured. They find it difficult to take part again in community life. They miss out on schooling and learning job skills. They are often forced into a life of crime.

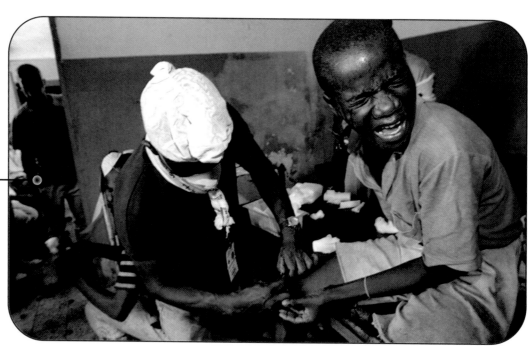

This child soldier has been wounded in a conflict in which he was forced to fight.

What countries use child soldiers to fight?

In 2001, there were conflicts in 37 countries where children were forced to fight and risk their lives.

Central and South Asia

- India
- Nepal
- Pakistan
- Tajikistan
- Uzbekistan

Middle East

- Afghanistan
- Iran
- Iraq
- Israel and occupied territories
- Lebanon

Africa

- Algeria
- Angola
- Burundi
- Chad
- Congo
- Democratic Republic of Congo
- Eritrea
- Ethiopia
- Liberia
- Rwanda
- Sierra Leone
- Somalia
- Sudan
- Uganda

Southeast Asia/Oceania

- Burma (Myanmar)
- East Timor
- Indonesia
- Papua New Guinea
- Philippines
- Solomon Islands

Central and South America

- Colombia
- El Salvador
- Mexico
- Peru

Europe

- Russian Federation
- Turkey
- Yugoslavia

Children forced from their homes

It is hard for many people to imagine what it would be like to:
- ◎ be forced to leave their country
- ◎ become homeless
- ◎ lose family and friends
- ◎ want to find a new place to live.

In the world today, more than 30 million people have been forced to run away from their homes because of war, bad treatment, or the threat of harm. Many of these people are children who become separated from their families. They often only have the clothes they are wearing and a few other belongings.

Asylum-seekers

detention centers places separated from the rest of the community where asylum-seekers are made to live

Asylum-seekers are children and adults who are forced to leave their home country. They travel to a safer place to stay until things get better or they are allowed to live in the new country. Many countries keep children and adults who are asylum-seekers in a group of buildings away from the rest of the community. These places are called detention centers. Detention centers are often surrounded with heavy metal fencing and guards watch everyone. In some countries, children asylum-seekers are locked up inside these centers until a decision is made about whether they and their families can stay in the new country.

These children asylum-seekers are playing inside a detention center.

Refugees

Refugees are children and adults who can never return to their homelands. They have been forced to leave and want to start new lives in safer countries. The countries that agree to take refugees accept them as new citizens. Most asylum-seekers are trying to prove that they are true refugees. They want to be accepted as citizens of a new country.

refugees
people who have been forced to leave their home countries and who are accepted to live in other countries

Many asylum-seekers live in camps like this one in Pakistan on the border of Afghanistan. They stay here and wait to see if other countries will take them in as refugees.

What can global citizens do to help?

There are ways that global citizens can help refugees:

◎ Collect donated goods that can be given to refugees when they settle in their new country.

◎ Ask your school, church, or local community group to adopt a refugee family. Welcome them. Spend time with them and help them settle into the neighborhood.

◎ Try to help them learn English by talking to them patiently. Explain what things mean in a simple way.

◎ The main thing is not to let them feel alone and cut off from the community. They are people and new citizens who deserve the same respect and care that we all do.

UNHCR
The UN Refugee Agency

What can I do?

I'm going to keep up to date with what's happening to the world's refugees. I'll use the Internet to visit the website of the United Nations High Commission on Refugees at <www.unhcr.org>. It's the international body that helps protect their rights.

The United Nations protects human rights

When the United Nations organization was formed in 1945, it asked for cooperation from the world's countries to bring peace and to protect human rights. There are now 191 member countries. They work together to:

◎ try to keep world peace and help solve differences
◎ build up friendly relationships between countries
◎ try to protect human rights
◎ provide meeting places for countries to discuss issues
◎ help countries in need.

The United Nations has a special section called the Commission on Human Rights. It checks on human rights in different countries.

Symbol of the United Nations

A declaration of human rights for all

In 1948, the United Nations made a document on human rights called the "Universal Declaration of Human Rights." It is called "universal" because it should apply to all people everywhere. It is called a "declaration" because it asks for agreement from countries. The document has 30 articles. Each article covers an aspect of human rights.

Most countries have signed the declaration, but it has not yet been made law everywhere.

articles
the separate parts of an important document

Mary Robinson was the United Nations High Commissioner for Human Rights from 1997–2002. Here she joins a special ceremony of school children planting symbolic red hands that ask the world to ban child soldiers.

UNIVERSAL DECLARATION OF HUMAN RIGHTS

1. Children are born free and should be treated equally.
2. Everyone has the right to everything in this declaration regardless of background and beliefs.
3. People have the right to live in freedom and safety.
4. Nobody has the right to make someone a slave.
5. Nobody has the right to hurt anyone.
6. Rights should be protected in all countries of the world.
7. The law should be the same for everyone.
8. A person can ask for help from the law if their rights are not protected.
9. Nobody has the right to put someone in prison, or to send them away from their country, without a good reason.
10. Trials should be done in public.
11. A person is innocent until it can be proved that they are guilty.
12. Nobody can harm a person's good name, enter their house, open their letters, or bother them without a good reason.
13. People can come and go as they wish within their country.
14. If someone hurts another person because of what they believe in, they can go to another country and ask for protection.
15. People have the right to belong to a country that they choose.
16. A person of legal age can marry and have a family. Men and women have the same rights when they are married.
17. A person has the right to own things. Nobody has the right to take these things away without good reason.
18. People have the right to choose their religion, to change it, and to practice it.
19. People have the right to think what they want and to say what they like.
20. People have the right to take part in meetings in a peaceful way, but nobody can force a person to belong to a group.
21. People have the right to choose politicians by voting freely for their choice. Men and women have equal votes.
22. A person has the right to grow and to make the most of all things in their community.
23. People have the right to work and to get a wage that allows them to support a family. If a man and a woman do the same work, they should get the same pay.
24. Each workday should not be too long. Everyone has the right to rest and should be able to take regular paid vacations.
25. People have the right to what they need so that they and their families do not get sick, are not cold, and have shelter. They have the right to be helped if they need it. All children have the same rights even if their parents are not married.
26. Everyone has the right to go to school. Primary schooling should be free. Parents have the right to choose how and what their children will be taught at school.
27. The works of an artist, writer, or a scientist should be protected. They should be able to earn money and respect from them.
28. There should be a law that can fully protect these rights and freedoms so that human rights are respected in all countries of the world.
29. Each person has responsibilities towards others in their community.
30. In all parts of the world, no society or person can destroy the rights and freedoms contained in this declaration.

The main points of the Universal Declaration of Human Rights are summarized here in easy-to-read language.

Rights for women

Human rights are for all people. However, in certain communities, women do not have equal rights with men, and girls do not have equal rights with boys, such as:

◎ Women often have to work for much less pay than men for the same sort of work.
◎ There are some good jobs that women are not allowed to hold just because they are female.
◎ Women can be expected to do all of the household work and also work outside the house, such as in farm fields or factories.
◎ Girls are made to leave school very early to look after younger brothers and sisters, or sick parents and grandparents. They do not get the same opportunities as boys to learn the skills to get good jobs later in their lives.
◎ Women are often not allowed to own land or houses.
◎ War can leave women without husbands and sons to help support the family. The women and their young children could be forced out of their homes and onto the streets with few things of their own.

exploit
to use selfishly and for personal gain

Everyone has the right to work. Sometimes this right is exploited. Sometimes women have to work long days on farms but also do all the household work.

The right to paid work

Article 23 of the "Universal Declaration of Human Rights" says that all people over the age of 15 should be able to go to work. They should be paid enough money for their work to support the basic needs of a family.

Another side of the right to work is that people who own businesses or are managers should not exploit workers. Owners exploit workers if wages are low, working hours long, and conditions poor. This makes poor workers stay poor. This creates a gap between the rich and the poor.

Rights for minority groups

Human rights are for everyone, regardless of their race, social background, or physical ability. There are groups in most communities that have special things in common. They form only a small part of the main population. These are called minority groups.

Indigenous peoples

There are about 350 million indigenous people in more than 70 countries around the globe. Over the past 500 years, the human rights of indigenous people in many areas of the world have been harmed. New settlers in their lands used violence and force to become the main culture. They took the land from the indigenous groups and tried to destroy their cultures.

Full human rights for indigenous groups would allow them to have their own cultures, languages, and land.

minority groups
groups of people who are different from the main population in things like language, culture, and ability

indigenous people
groups with the same language and culture who are related to the first people in an area

People with disabilities

Many of the world's people live with physical or mental disabilities. A disabled person has some type of permanent injury that prevents them acting to their full capacity. They could have become disabled:
◎ at birth
◎ through an illness or accident
◎ in a war zone.

In some communities, disabled people are treated unfairly. Their human rights are limited because they do not fit easily into daily life.

Indigenous people want to protect their rights. This person from an indigenous group in South America takes part in a meeting about their rights.

Physical disabilities should not limit people's right to work.

25

Why do wars occur?

Conflict is a normal part of our daily lives. We all have disagreements with others where we try to get them to change their points of view. But conflict can get out of hand and become violent. A conflict becomes a war when it is violent. Two or more groups use weapons to kill each other and destroy property.

Today's wars

Wars today are often civil wars. A civil war is quite different to what you read in books or see on TV about wars between countries that are fought across borders.

Civil wars:

◎ are fought within nations instead of across borders
◎ often occur between a government army and a group who does not want the government to rule
◎ kill civilians and destroy whole villages.

One hundred years ago, 9 out of 10 people who died were soldiers. Today, only 2 out of 10 victims are soldiers. The other 8 out of 10 are civilians.

civil wars
wars between different groups within the same country

civilians
people who do not belong to any defense forces

In 2001, more than 40 wars were being fought in 37 countries.

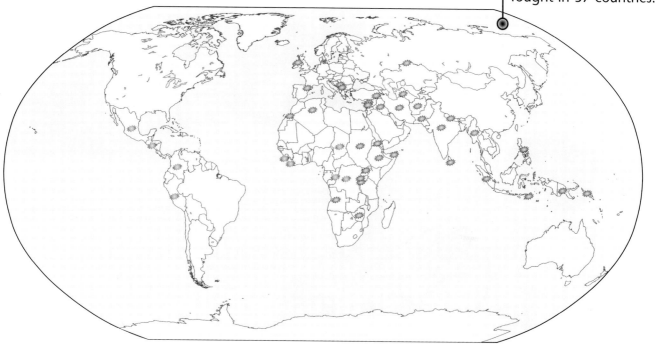

Effects of war

War affects everyone, not just the soldiers fighting. Many civilians are killed or injured. Even aid workers and people from the media can be victims.

Children are more at risk than adults in war. War can destroy children's rights in many ways:

◎ They often cannot go to school during war.
◎ They could be forced to leave their homes as refugees. While fleeing, they can become separated from their parents.
◎ One or both parents could die in conflict.
◎ Families cannot plant crops because of fighting or landmines. This leads to a lack of food.
◎ Many are left homeless because houses and property are destroyed.
◎ They can be injured and left disabled.
◎ They could be forced to become soldiers.

Many of these effects also apply to adults. Their human rights can also be destroyed if civilians are put in prison or are tortured.

War destroys human rights, especially those of children.

What can I do?

It costs a lot to make a landmine, but it costs 10 times more to remove one. In some countries, about 30 percent of landmine victims lose one or both legs. I'm going to make a poster to put up at school. It will show how landmines affect civilian rights.

Peaceful choices

There are ways of solving conflicts that do not use violence or force. These are peaceful ways. Peace does not mean that we should just sit back and hope for calm. Global citizens use peaceful actions to solve problems. In 1947, Mahatma Gandhi, a peace leader in India said a very important thing:

"There is no way to peace. Peace is the way."

Peaceful protest marching is a way of global citizens getting together to bring attention to a war. The media covers such public protests so other people who do not take part can read about it or watch it.

The symbols of peace

Different symbols of peace are used and recognized around the world. Wherever you see these symbols, you know that people are acting for peace and human rights.

Different symbols are used to mean peace.

What can I do?

Just saying no to violence, and meaning it, is one of the best ways to act for peace.

28

Global citizens work for peace

There have always been people who work for peace. They try to make others see that there are peaceful solutions to problems.

reconciliation
understanding and agreement

 Three world peace workers

Mahatma Gandhi, India
Mahatma Gandhi was born in 1869 near Mumbai in India. He studied law then went to work in South Africa. He became involved in a struggle for the rights of non-white people. When he returned to India, he set up a peaceful community based on honest work where everyone had equal rights. Gandhi started peaceful actions to help the Indian people. After 1947, he worked very hard to try to bring peace between Indian Hindus and Muslims from Pakistan. He was shot and killed in 1948 by a fellow Hindu who thought that Gandhi was betraying the Hindus by wanting peaceful reconciliation with Muslims.

Martin Luther King Jr., U.S.
Martin Luther King Jr. won the 1964 Nobel Peace Prize. At that time, African-Americans had to obey segregation laws. They had to give up their seat in a bus to white passengers even if they were tired or pregnant.

King's struggle for equal rights was based on the message of brotherly love. He based a lot of his peaceful action on the thinking of Gandhi.

He was assassinated on April 4, 1968. In the U.S., the third Monday in January each year is a national holiday for Martin Luther King Jr. Day.

segregation
an official law that isolated black and colored people from white people

Mother Teresa, India
Mother Teresa worked as a Roman Catholic missionary in India from 1929 until she died in 1997. She devoted her life to working for the poor in the slums of Calcutta. With volunteers and money aid, she started her own order in 1950 called "The Missionaries of Charity." Their main task was to love and care for the people that nobody else would look after.

Today, the order has more than 1,000 sisters and brothers in India. Many have been trained as doctors, nurses, and social workers. They give help to the slum population as well as undertaking relief work in connection with natural disasters.

Mother Teresa won the Nobel Peace Prize in 1979. She is expected to be made a saint by the Catholic Church.

Action for human rights

We are all citizens of the world. But some of us are more active than others. Global citizens put their ideas into action. Some people think that "action" means protesting or doing something violent. But action can take many forms and can always be peaceful, even in a protest march.

These are some of the actions that global citizens can take to help make a difference:

◎ thinking deeply about issues
◎ volunteering and participating in community activities
◎ helping out wherever you can
◎ standing up for others
◎ joining others on a Web site to lodge petitions with governments
◎ discussing and solving problems in peaceful ways.

Global citizens can make a difference so that more people's human rights are respected. Remember: an idea is only an idea until someone puts it into action.

What can we do?

The peace activist Elise Bjorn–Hansen Boulding says that there won't be a better world unless we IMAGINE it first. We're going to IMAGINE that by the time we're 50 there will be human rights for all. People will solve problems peacefully. Our environment will be recovering from all the damage people caused it over the past 300 years. We are going to IMAGINE that, as she said, "Humans had learned to listen to one another and to the planet."

articles the separate parts of an important document

child labor where children under 15 are forced to work for low pay and in bad conditions

citizen a person who lives in a large group of people who they mix with

civilians people who do not belong to any defense forces

civil wars wars between different groups within the same country

conflict violent disagreement

convention a document that countries agree to and must make the law

declaration a document that countries agree to but do not have to make law

detention centers places separated from the rest of the community where asylum-seekers are made to live

dignity respecting yourself

environments natural and built surroundings

exploit to use selfishly and for personal gain

freedom the right to choose

generation people of about the same age group and living at the same time

gender whether a person is male (boy, man) or female (girl, woman)

human rights the basic claims that all people have to fair, safe, and comfortable lives

indigenous people groups with the same language and culture who are related to the first people in an area

international worldwide

landmines bombs that have been hidden in the earth that will explode when stepped on

law rules that must be obeyed

malnutrition an illness caused by not having enough healthy food

minority groups groups of people who are different from the main population in things like language, culture, and ability

needs the things that people must have to stay alive

overcrowding a large number of people living in a very small area in cramped conditions

politics the groups who control and run a country

pollution dirty or dangerous conditions that make a part of the environment unclean or unsafe

poverty extreme lack of money or wealth

reconciliation understanding and agreement

refugees people who have been forced to leave their home countries and who are accepted to live in other countries

responsibilities duties that have to be done

rights fair claims to things in daily life

sanitation clean and safe removal of human waste by water and drains

segregation an official law that isolated black and colored people from white people

self-esteem the feelings a person has about their own value

shanty town an area of very poor housing conditions next to better housing in a city

shelter a place, like a house, that gives people protection from the weather

slaves people who are owned by another, have no freedom, and must obey the owner

standard of living everyday living conditions in a community

starvation suffering or death because of lack of food

torture extreme cruelty

United Nations a worldwide organization that aims to protect peace and human rights

wants the things that people like to have to make their life comfortable, but are not essential